16.95

W9-AXJ-329

How Roads Are Made

Text   Owen Williams
Design   Eddie Poulton

Contents

Facts On File
New York • Oxford

All Kinds of Roads

The word "roads" may bring to mind the road to school, the road to work or, perhaps, the road on a trip. All these roads may be of different types, from the smallest farm road to the largest multilane highway. They have in common, however, the same purpose – the easy and economical movement of people. Roads enable cities, towns, villages, factories and farms to be linked with each other. They make it possible for the natural resources of a country to be developed. They bring people together.

The 20th century – particularly during the last fifty years – has seen the extensive building of roads throughout the world. This dramatic expansion has, of course, been brought about by the development of the motor vehicle, which has become progressively more economical and reliable, simpler to drive, and more varied in use.

The chart below shows the enormous increase in the number of vehicles in use worldwide. As traffic increases, so more and more roads are needed. In country areas, and in towns that have a low density of traffic, single-lane roads with "at grade" intersections are adequate. Most roads are of this type. For the higher volumes of traffic in and between towns, divided highways with two, three, and occasionally more, traffic lanes in each direction are needed. Where traffic is at its heaviest, separation of roads from pedestrians is essential, to ensure maximum safety and controlled traffic flow. This need is fulfilled by the "grade-separated" road, which passes over or under other roads and by grade-separated interchanges.

This book explains how roads are planned, designed and built and how traffic volumes and weight, terrain and climate determine their type and construction.

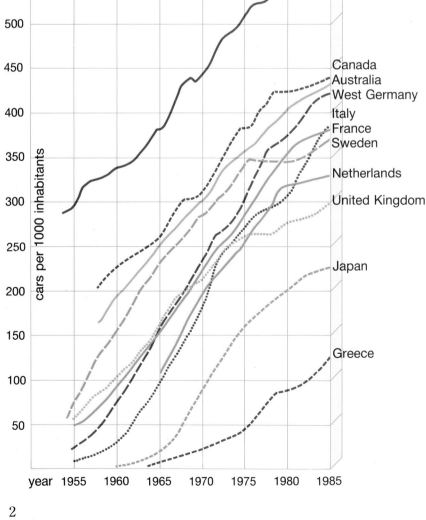

Opposite. Two contrasting types of modern road. (Above) Expressways in a highly developed urban area (Chicago). Notice how the expressways (center left and foreground) are constructed below ground level so that the extensive local road system may be carried over them on bridges, minimizing interference with property. (Below) An unpaved road in a rural area of Kenya.

Right. The Appian Way, parts of which are still in use. Notice the pavement surface of stone slabs retained at the sides by large stone blocks.

Below. Network of Roman roads in Europe (circa 1st century A.D.) for pedestrian and horse drawn traffic. The most important roads were paved, as shown in the photograph of the Appian Way above. Compare this with the map below of the Interstate Highway System in the US, which provides facilities for rapid transport by motor vehicles.

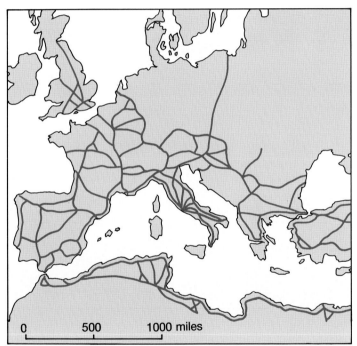

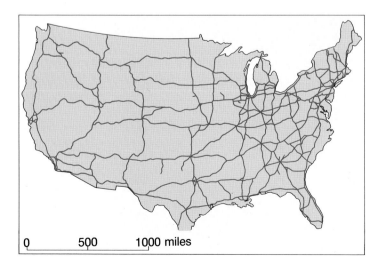

History

The first roads were little more than well-traveled tracks, beaten out by the feet of men and the hooves of horses or camels. The first well-documented description of road engineering dates back to Roman times. The Romans constructed a network of over 52,000 miles of road throughout Europe, linking Rome to its centers of supply. The roads had **geometrical alignments**, carefully constructed **pavements**, and well-designed drainage. In Europe today, some highways – such as the Fosse Way in England and the Appian Way in Italy – still follow the old Roman routes.

By the Middle Ages, the Roman techniques of road building had been largely forgotten, and roads gradually fell into decay. It is of interest, however, that when the Spanish Conquistadors arrived in Peru in the early 1500s they found that the Incas already had an extensive road system. Today, the remains of a road some 1,200 miles long between Quito and Cuzco attest to the magnificence of its construction in the wild and mountainous regions of the High Andes.

In Europe it was not until the 1700s, by which time roads generally were in an appalling state, that the principles of modern road design and construction began to be studied once more. In 1720 the Corps des Ingénieurs des Ponts et Chaussées was formed in France for this purpose.

東海道五拾三次之内
吉原
左富士

In Britain in the late 1700s and early 1800s, the work of three remarkable engineers, Thomas Telford, John Metcalf and John McAdam, was mainly responsible for the development of standards in road design and construction – particularly in the fields of alignment, gradient, pavement and drainage. Although their roads were designed for stagecoaches and other such traffic, their works have stood up to the test of time. For example, Telford's work (1815-1822) on the Shrewsbury to Holyhead Road, which runs through the rugged country of North Wales, is a model of its time and is still used by traffic today.

With the advent of the railways in the 1800s, interest in roads declined, but the development of the motorcar in the early 1900s brought about a revival. In the 1920s and 1930s in the US and Europe new types of road specially designed for motor traffic were introduced – the most revolutionary being the Italian Autostrada and the German Autobahn.

The last fifty years has seen the development throughout the world not only of extensive stretches of specialized highway, but of all types of road catering to many different needs. A remarkable example of this development is the interstate highway system in the US.

(Above) Illustration from one of Ando Hiroshige's *53 Stations of the Tokaido*, 1833-34. At that time the Tokaido was the principal artery of communications between eastern and western Honshu, Japan. Compare it with the illustration below of a section of the Tomei Expressway, a part of Japan's extensive modern expressway system.

The Stages of Road Making

If you have seen a road being made you may have thought about the benefits that it will bring to the local community or the changes that it will make to the environment. A road construction site sometimes appears to be rather quiet, with little sign of activity. Then, again, it can look very dramatic, with heavy machinery such as diggers and rippers excavating **cuttings**, and building **embankments** and bridges. It is an expensive process, too, but the costs do not end when the road is opened to traffic. The management and maintenance of the road have to be paid for while it is in use, which may be for many years to come.

However, the actual construction is the last of many stages in making a road. A great deal of thought has to be given to how necessary a proposed road would be, now and in the future; the planning and design of the road; how much it would cost to build and maintain; the benefits it would bring; and the effect it would have on the

social environment and landscape.

To deal with these issues, the Road Authority carries out the project in a series of stages.

First, the road authority has to make sure that there is a need for the road. If there is, it then has to find the best route that the road should take. Preliminary studies will produce several possible routes, each of which has to be examined by engineers and assessed for traffic use and benefits, construction and land purchase costs, and the effects on the environment and landscape. Consultations are held with government and other authorities whose interests may be involved.

As a result of the studies, the number of route options are narrowed down. The plans are often exhibited to the public for their consideration and comment. Having taken notes of their various objections or views, the road authority then has to decide which of the options

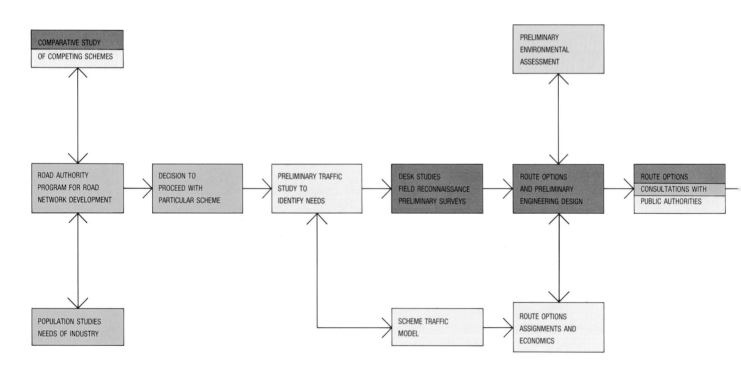

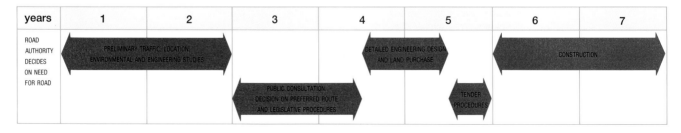

6

to adopt as its preferred route.

People who may be affected by the chosen route – for instance a farmer through whose land the road might run – will have the chance to put forward their objections at an independent public hearing. This can result in alterations being made to the route or even in its rejection. It is only when a preferred route has passed successfully through all the stages that the road authority can obtain the legal powers to proceed with the land purchase for the **right-of-way**, and the construction.

The details of the road's engineering design now have to be completed. Usually, the construction is carried out by contractors, so the road authority has to ensure that the contractors are given the correct instructions on which to base their bids for the job. Schedules of materials, which list the various construction operations and materials involved, and plans, specifications and Bidding Sheets are prepared.

These documents and the engineering drawings and specifications are given to selected civil engineering contractors, so that they can work out the cost of construction. The firm that enters the lowest bid normally wins the contract.

Once the contract has been awarded, the preliminary stages of making a road have been completed. The problems of construction now have to be sorted out by the contractor. They include the techniques and methods to be used, the sequence of operations, the hiring and managing of the work force, the delivery of machinery and materials to the site – which can be difficult until the road is built – and coping with bad weather.

Despite all of the problems, the construction is often the shortest stage in road making. It is the work that has gone on behind the scenes before construction starts at the site that is time-consuming. Many people will have been involved in all the different aspects of road making – administration, law, economics, traffic, design, environmental studies – to ensure that the route options have been thoroughly examined, that the civil engineering design is correct, and that the road is located where it is needed with the least negative effect on the environment.

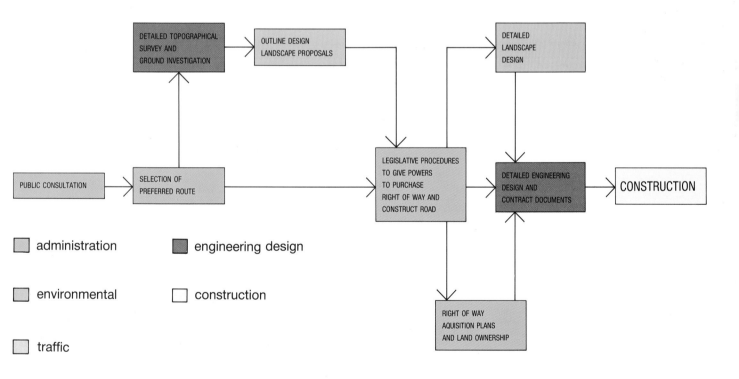

This chart illustrates the sequence of activities leading to construction of a road in a developed area where it will affect many existing interests. The diagram left shows a likely time scale for the completion of these activities.

Traffic

Traffic is what roads are all about. The amount of traffic you find on a road varies from a single-lane rural road used infrequently to a multilane highway in constant use. So, when a new road is being designed, the first problem to think about is the volume and type of traffic that it will be expected to carry: cars, buses, trucks. This will determine the type of road required, the number of traffic lanes that it will need, and whether the cost can be justified in terms of the benefits to road users and to society in general. To plan a bigger road than is needed would be a waste of money, and too small a road would result in traffic congestion.

It is not an easy decision to make. The first step is to examine available road traffic data and road conditions in the existing road network, asking the question, "by how much has the traffic increased over the years and will it continue to grow?" Methods used to find the answers are mechanical counts, manual counts and surveys of where traffic is coming from and going to.

Mechanical counts
Occasionally you may have noticed a thin rubber tube stretched across a road. This operates a pneumatic device that records the number of axles driving over it. It gives an approximate number of vehicles using the road, but it cannot record the difference between a car and a truck.

Manual counts
These are carried out by people counting vehicles as they pass. The "census personnel", as they are called, may also note the different types of vehicle, the number of people in a vehicle, and where it turns off the road.

Surveys
This method involves stopping a selected number of vehicles and asking the drivers where they started their journey, where they are going, and the reason for their journey: business or pleasure. If a series of surveys are carried out at several locations, they give a clear picture of the routes that will be needed.

The three methods produce data on current traffic volumes. If the counts are made on a regular basis they can be compared to assess traffic growth over the years. They will also show if an increase in traffic is due to a new development specific to the area: for instance, a

A manual traffic survey in progress under police control in an outlying district of a small town (St. Denis, Réunion in the Indian Ocean).

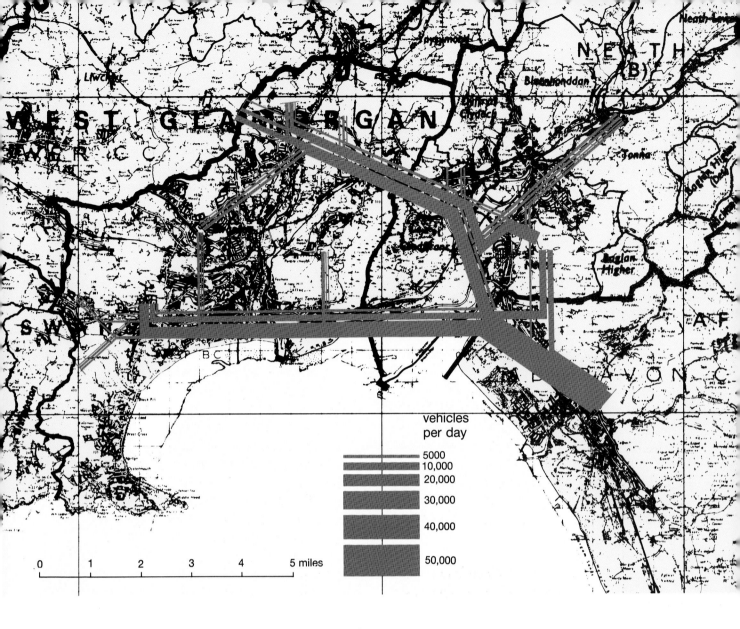

vehicles
per day

	5000
	10,000
	20,000
	30,000
	40,000
	50,000

0   1   2   3   4   5 miles

A diagrammatic illustration of traffic volume (vehicles per day) and
distribution, derived from a traffic study.

new housing complex.

When this information is fed into a
computer, a mathematical model can be made
that will predict how the introduction of a new
road will affect the existing network, and how
much traffic will be attracted to it. Any future
planned development and social or economic
changes have to be taken into consideration
too. The road itself may help to make the
changes. For example, it may attract industry to
the area.

To be realistic the traffic forecast can only
look ahead up to a maximum of fifteen years
and it is only as good as the information and
assumptions on which it is based.

The next questions to think about are
where to locate the new road, how it should
be connected to the existing network, and what
type of road it needs to be to accommodate

the forecasted average daily flow of traffic or
– particularly in the case of urban roads –
rush-hour flow.

A **design speed** will then have to be
selected for the road. This is the expected
top speed of the traffic which will be using the
road (30, 50 or 70 mph). For economic reasons
this is related to the terrain through which the
road passes. For example, it would probably
be too expensive to build a 70 mph-standard
road through mountains. Then, for each design,
speed and type of road, certain standards of
alignment have to be provided – **gradient**,
curves, **sight lines** and **sight stopping
distance** – to make sure that the road will be
safe, with an even flow of traffic.

When all this information has been collated,
the next stage – route location options – can be
tackled.

Route Location

Roads can be built in a wide variety of locations – through the middle of a city, across rolling country or mountains, or in a desert – presenting a wide scope for the civil engineer's skills, which are used to plan, design and construct a road.

Wherever a road is built the objective is to find a route that meets alignment standards and reduces the operating costs of the traffic, brings benefits to society and outweighs the cost of construction, maintenance and disturbance to the environment.

The two points between which the road will be located are fixed at the early planning stage. The route taken between the two points depends on geographical features, land use, developments and the need for intermediate connections to an existing road system. Having taken these factors into consideration, the civil engineer may still have several route options left, each of which might have different construction costs, a different attraction to traffic, and a different environmental impact.

For instance, it might cost more to dig a tunnel through a hill than it would to make the road longer by building it around the hill, but the shorter route through the tunnel might attract more traffic and cost less to maintain.

To begin with, a study is made of existing maps, geological information, the uses of land,

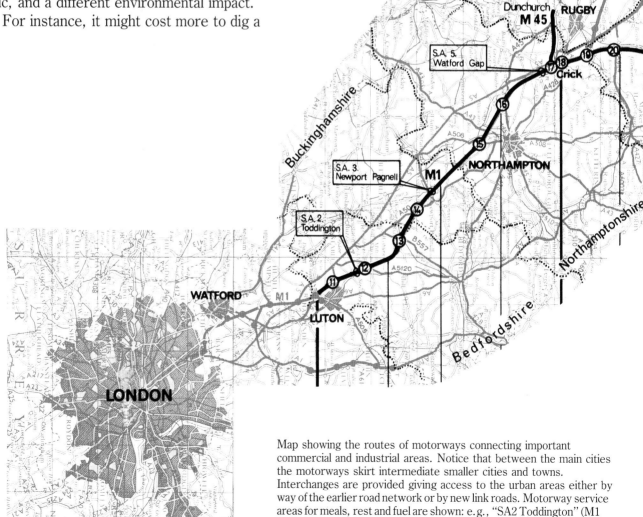

Map showing the routes of motorways connecting important commercial and industrial areas. Notice that between the main cities the motorways skirt intermediate smaller cities and towns. Interchanges are provided giving access to the urban areas either by way of the earlier road network or by new link roads. Motorway service areas for meals, rest and fuel are shown: e.g., "SA2 Toddington" (M1 & M6 Motorways, UK).

and development plans, to help to decide on route "corridors." Then a reconnaissance field study is carried out to produce **topographical** and **geotechnical** information, which will narrow down the route options to be selected for final study and evaluation.

have to be dug out to make the cuttings or filled in to create embankments, and produce route plans to scale.

Armed with this information, the civil engineer can begin to think about the technical problems he may encounter with each route

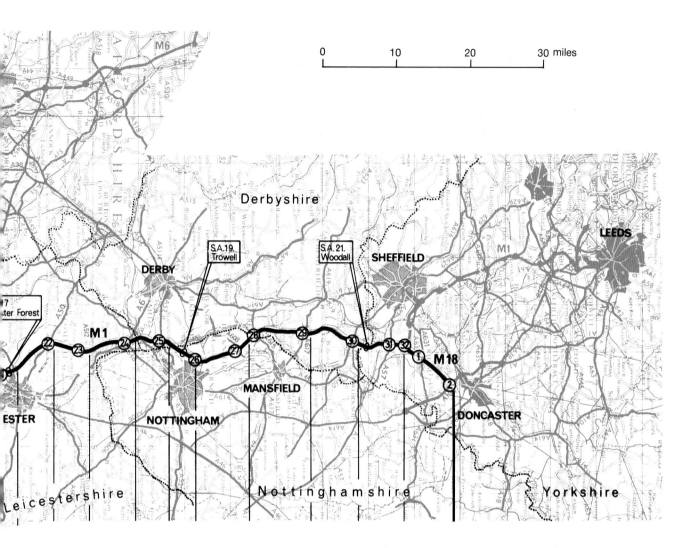

The final route option study contains very full topographic and geotechnical information. As more detailed information becomes available, the study is refined and evaluated until the route options can be listed in order of their cost and economic return. The possible effect on the environment cannot be measured in terms of money but it has to be considered at this stage.

Field and desk studies involve a large amount of data and **geometric computation**, so the computer is an essential tool for the civil engineer. When the topographic information is fed into the computer special software enables the data to to stored as a digital ground model (DGM). Then, given the geometry for each route, the program will provide the computations for the alignment, calculate how much land will

option. He will have to decide:
– How the ground will behave when the cuttings are excavated or the embankments are made. For example, will the earth slip?
– Will the earth and other materials dug out of the ground be suitable for making embankments and will it be an equal amount?
– If not, where will they be able to deposit the extra material, or where can they find the extra earth to make the embankment?
– How will ground conditions affect pavement design?
– How will rivers and their flood plains, existing roads, railways and canals affect the route?
– What structures will be needed: e.g., bridges, viaducts, **retaining walls**, tunnels?
– How much will it all cost?

11

Topographical Survey

The location of a new road depends to a great extent on the **topography** of the land. This is why a topographical survey, which measures and records the form of the earth's surface and the physical features on it, is carried out.

In open country, the survey will enable the road engineer to find the road alignment that fits best into the **ground form**, keeping earthworks to a minimum. In urban areas, a survey helps to determine the route that can thread through built-up areas with the minimum of disturbance to houses, shops, and other amenities.

Traditionally, topographical surveys are carried out by making measurements on the ground, using a **theodolite**. A theodolite measures the angles from which the position of ground features can be calculated. **Surveyor's levels** are used to obtain ground heights and chains and tapes to measure the shorter distances. Using this information, maps and plans can be drawn to scale.

Today, topographical surveys are more often carried out from the air. To make maps and plans, aerial surveyors use special techniques in which pairs of photographs of the ground are taken from aircraft, using a specialized camera. The photos are put in a **stereo plotter**,

Taking aerial photographs from a survey aircraft.

Below. Diagram showing the principle of aerial survey. The photographs must overlap. The overlapped areas can then be viewed stereoscopically, giving a three-dimensional picture of the area, from which accurate mapping can be made.

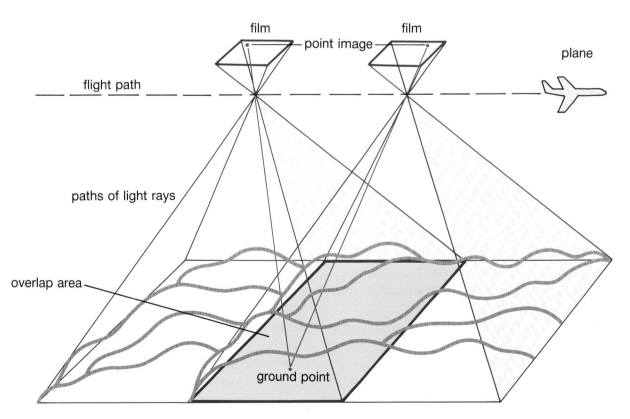

Surveyors using an EDM instrument to check control stations on the alignment of a new motorway.

which scans features selected by the operators and records them in digital form.

An air survey has some advantages over the traditional ground survey. It takes less time over larger areas, minimizes the problem of access to the area, and provides a pictorial record of the ground at the time of the survey.

However, the areas in which ground surveys can compete with air surveys are increasing, due to improvements in technology. Electronic theodolites, distance measuring equipment (EDM's) and data recorders have helped to speed up ground surveys and to make them easier.

An electronic theodolite contains a micro-processor that displays corrected readings in digital form.

With the **EDM system**, a prism is set up as a target over the feature to be surveyed. Then an **infrared ray** – or **microwaves** if the distance to be measured is very long – is beamed to the prism, which reflects the beam back to the EDM instrument, enabling it to compute the distance.

The EDM equipment can either be built into a theodolite, or attached to it (rather like a camera flash) when both distance and angle measurements are required. The measurements are stored electronically in a data logger and they can then be down-loaded directly into a computer for processing.

Whichever of the two survey methods is used, ground or aerial, first of all a network of **trigonometrical stations** – points of known position and height – has to be established on the ground. Using these stations, the positions of physical features, for instance a hill, can be fixed by measurement on the ground or interpreted from aerial photographs. The positions of public utility services – gas, electricity, telephone, drains, water pipes etc. – are located and noted.

From the information gathered in the topographical survey, maps and plans are made on which the route options can be studied. Finally, the detailed design of the preferred route is prepared.

Computers are used to store the maps and plans in a **Digital Ground Model (DGM)**. The computer program then combines the DGM with the principal geometry of the road alignment and the road's standards – widths, slopes, and so on – to produce detailed geometry of the route and calculations of the earthwork quantities. Using plotting equipment, the computer also produces the survey maps and plans, with the road, its cuttings, embankments and boundaries superimposed on them.

13

Geological Survey and Soil Testing

A geological study and a soil survey are carried out to discover the characteristics of the soils and rocks that will be encountered during construction. The road design and construction methods depend upon the following information:

Type: rock, gravel, sand, silt, clay or mixtures of them;
Origin: volcanic, marine, **lacustrine**, glacial, water-borne, wind-blown;
Strength, compressibility and *strata sequence.*

A study of geological conditions can often begin by examining existing geological maps and records of earlier engineering works with, where possible, a **walkover survey**. In underdeveloped areas these facts may not be available, so the study has to begin from scratch. On major projects, air survey and satellite photography can help.

The more detailed examination of the geology may include studies of the area's:

Geomorphology
By looking at the shapes and contours of the area a great deal of information can be gleaned about sub-surface movements and unstable slopes.

Hydrology
The water content of the ground and its movement (flow).

Stratigraphy
Borings are taken across the area to find out how the soil or rock is layered.

Lithology
A study is made of the physical properties of the various rocks and soils to determine their probable behavior in cuttings and embankments and to discover whether they can be used as foundations for bridges and pavements.

Mineralogy
This study will identify possible sources of **aggregates** for concrete construction and for use as road stone.

When the geological study is complete

A simple tripod rig for extracting soil samples.

Examination in the laboratory of continuous core rock samples obtained by drilling into rock strata.

it reveals whether the geology of the area is uniform, or whether it is more complex. Taking into account the nature of the planned construction, this will determine the scope of the soil survey and the methods of carrying it out. The most common method is to examine the soils by taking borings and by digging trial pits at selected sites on the route. The type of soil found at various depths is recorded and samples are carefully extracted for a closer look in the laboratory where they are compared with the geological information. Then they are classified and tested under standard test procedures.

In some surveys geophysical methods of detecting the underlying strata can be used, avoiding the need for extensive boring. For example, if it is planned to dig to bedrock along the route, there is no need to take samples of the soil lying on top of it. Similarly, in some soils where the type and consistency are already known, strength tests at varying depths can be carried out quickly on the spot.

Some examples of why the geotechnical properties of the soils and rocks, disclosed by the soil survey, are so important are:

Cuttings

The survey will establish the slopes that are safe and stable enough for excavation. If a slope is unstable, a landslide could occur. This can be avoided by using flatter slopes or by installing drainage.

Embankments

An embankment is man-made and, as material is loaded onto it, it begins to compress. The soil study indicates the total **settlement** and rate of settlement of the soils. Soft soils that retain water take an unacceptable time to settle, especially if settlement continues long after construction. In some cases the settlement can be accelerated by special drainage or by overbuilding the height of the embankment.

If the soils are very weak – like those found in marshlands – they may be replaced with better materials to form the foundation of the embankment; or a structural solution such as a viaduct may have to be found.

Road pavement

The thickness of the road pavement needed to spread the traffic load depends on the strength of the soils below.

Structures

The survey helps the engineer to assess acceptable foundation pressures on the soils and their likely settlement rate and the intensity of soil, rock and hydraulic pressure loadings on retaining walls, bridge abutments and tunnels.

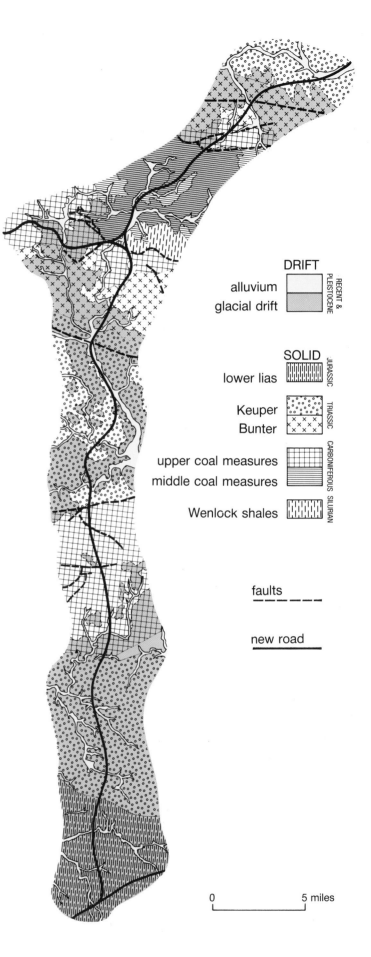

DRIFT

alluvium

glacial drift

RECENT & PLEISTOCENE

SOLID

lower lias — JURASSIC

Keuper
Bunter — TRIASSIC

upper coal measures
middle coal measures — CARBONIFEROUS

Wenlock shales — SILURIAN

faults

new road

0   5 miles

Map showing how the geology can vary along the route of a new road.

Earthworks

In road making the word "earthworks" is used to describe all the operations involved in the excavation of cuttings and the construction of embankments. The top surface of the earthworks is called the **formation** and it provides the foundation of the **road pavement**.

The formation has to follow accurately the lines and levels of the road alignment and it has to be strong enough to bear the traffic load that is imposed on it through the pavement.

The volumes of earthworks on a road vary according to the road's standards and the terrain. Typically, on a major modern six-lane divided road of a high standard situated in undulating terrain, some 350,000 tons of soil per mile might be excavated and transported.

It requires large machinery and skilled organization to excavate, transport and deposit such enormous quantities of material economically. The type of plant used depends on the type of soil to be excavated and on the "haul distance" – the distance from where it is excavated to where it is deposited. Scrapers can be used for short hauls of about a mile to transport soft soils and even for soft rocks if these have been broken up first by a **ripper**. For longer hauls and for harder rocks, which first have to be blasted, excavators and trucks are used.

Before cuttings can be excavated and embankments formed, the site has to be prepared.

First, the topsoil is removed and stacked for re-use to cover the new slopes of the cuttings and the embankments. If necessary, special drainage is constructed to protect the cutting slopes; if the soil is weak, embankment sites are treated to accelerate ground settlements and to limit them where possible to within construction time. Stream culverts are constructed across the road so that material can be hauled along the line of the road. If necessary, temporary bridges are built.

In the cuttings it is essential to prevent the soils from becoming waterlogged, so the cutting has to be excavated in such a way that it is self-draining at all times. If this cannot be arranged, pumps are installed.

In the embankments, the **fill** material is placed in thoroughly compacted layers no thicker than 10 inches (25 centimeters) to

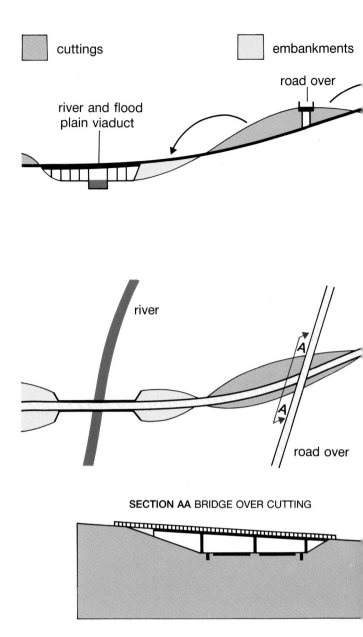

SECTION AA BRIDGE OVER CUTTING

avoid uneven settlement after completion and to reduce settlement to a minimum. In the laboratory, samples of soil from the site will have already undergone the **Proctor Test** – a standard compaction test. On site the standard compaction required is specified as a percentage of the Proctor Test.

When designing earthworks the aim is to balance the amount of material excavated for a cutting with the amount needed to fill embankments, without having to haul that material too far. However, it does not always work out as simply as that. Not all the excavated materials are suitable for use in embankments in their natural state because they may contain too much moisture. Methods do exist for improving the materials – treatment with lime or using alternate layers of other, free-draining material – but the cost of this has to be balanced against borrowing "fill" from elsewhere and removing

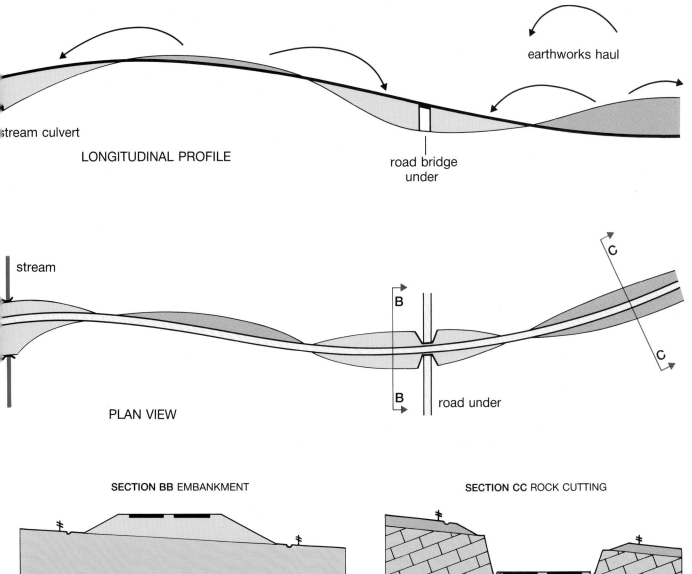

earthworks haul

stream culvert

LONGITUDINAL PROFILE

road bridge
under

stream

B

B

C

C

PLAN VIEW

road under

SECTION BB EMBANKMENT

SECTION CC ROCK CUTTING

Above. A diagrammatic illustration of some of the main features of a modern grade separated road passing through open rolling terrain. Notice how the provision of a smooth alignment for the road results in cuttings and embankments and the provision of culverts, bridges and viaducts.

Right. A rock cutting nearly 200 feet deep (Sydney to Newcastle Freeway, New South Wales, Australia).

the unsuitable material to waste disposal areas.

There is another factor that can affect the progress of earthworks: the climate. In areas where the soils are silt or clay, which retain water, operations have to be halted during wet weather – in countries with rainy seasons or monsoons for instance. On the other hand, in the drier areas – such as deserts – satisfactory compaction is impossible without watering the fill. In countries with colder climates, earthworks are generally not constructed during the winter.

Hydrology and Drainage

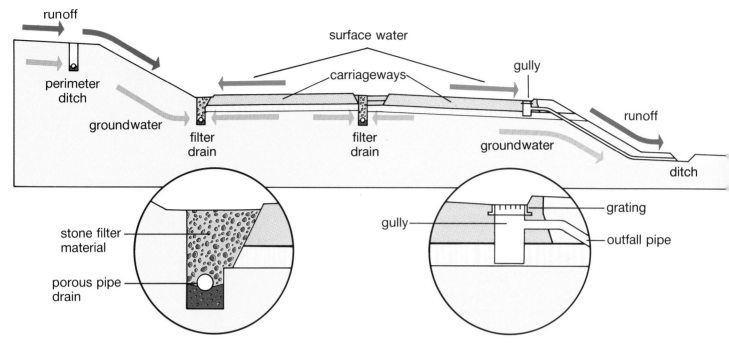

Diagram showing how the three kinds of water flow are controlled by drainage.

There are four reasons why a road must have a drainage system.

First, a natural drainage pattern already exists in the terrain before the road is built, and the pattern must not be destroyed. This means that if the road is to cross streams, rivers, or floodplains, structures such as bridges must be wide enough to allow flood flows to pass under them.

Second, the earthworks have to be protected from damage caused by water flowing either underground or overland from adjoining land.

Third, rain falling on the surface of the road pavement and earthworks has to be carried along to suitable discharge points in the natural drainage pattern.

Fourth, water levels in the ground beneath the road pavement have to be controlled in order to maintain the strength of the soils supporting the road pavement.

It is essential, therefore, to understand fully the hydrology of the area through which the road will pass.

Natural drainage pattern

Where major rivers have to be crossed, the most suitable crossing point will often become a fixed point on the route. A study of the flood flows will affect the extent and design of the structures crossing rivers and floodplains.

The accuracy of this study depends a great deal on the amount of historical data available about rainfall and past flood conditions. If this data does not exist, it may be necessary to set up field stations to collect river-flow and rainfall data.

The introduction of bridge piers and approach embankments into a waterway also has to be thought about. They can cause water levels to rise upstream making the water travel at a faster speed by the time it reaches the bridge. Physical or computer models help to predict the water level and flow.

Structures built across watercourses vary in size, from piped, box or arched culverts across smaller streams, to single or multi-span bridges for the larger rivers and long, multi-span viaducts across an extensive floodplain; where the water level can differ considerably between dry weather and floods.

Rainfall collection system

Water that runs off adjoining land can erode the cutting slopes, particularly if they consist of sandy soils or lack sufficient vegetation to help bind the soil. For instance, in arid regions, where soils are often sandy, an occasional heavy storm can cause great damage.

To avoid this, ditches are normally constructed at the top of cuttings before excavation to intercept the overland water and to direct it to the nearest watercourse.

If surface water collects on a road pavement it is a hazard to traffic, or if it drains through to the subsoil it weakens the foundation on which the road pavement has been constructed. A common way of preventing this from happening is to construct the road on a low embankment with ditches on either side to carry the water away. The shoulders and slopes of the embankment are constructed in such a way that they are not eroded by the water runoff.

The ditch system can be carried through cuttings, but if they are deep, or if the extra land needed in which to construct the system is not available, a closed pipe or channel system is built. To calculate the pipe or channel sizes requires knowledge of rainfall intensities in the area. However, some flooding due to exceptional storms also has to be allowed for.

Groundwater control

Water that flows underground is very important where the stability of cutting slopes is concerned, as it can weaken the soil, so the need for drainage is considered in the geotechnical design of the slopes.

If the strength of the ground below the road pavement is not sensitive to moisture, very little drainage is needed to collect the water draining through the pavement. On the other hand, if the ground is the type that does retain water, a method of drainage is provided – usually open-jointed or perforated **pipes**, surrounded by gravel and laid in trenches along the edges of the road pavement. The pipes are laid at the depth necessary to keep water well below the pavement construction, according to the type of soil to be drained.

Above. Viaduct carrying the road over a river bed which has dried out during the dry season but would flood in the wet season (Seeb to Niywa Road, Oman, in the Middle East).

Right. A typical corrugated steel pipe culvert designed to take a small stream or drainage under a road.

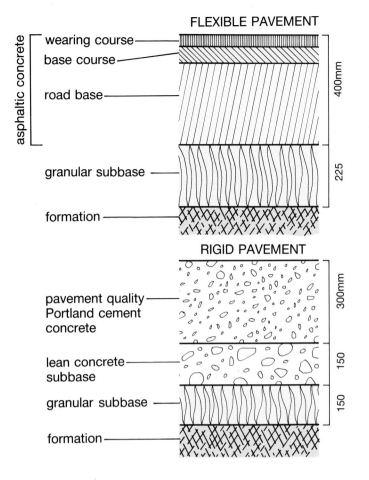

FLEXIBLE PAVEMENT

asphaltic concrete
- wearing course
- base course
- road base

400mm

granular subbase

225

formation

RIGID PAVEMENT

pavement quality Portland cement concrete

300mm

lean concrete subbase

150

granular subbase

150

formation

Left. The construction layers of typical "flexible" and "rigid" pavements.

The Road Pavement

A road pavement has two purposes. The first is to distribute the pressure loadings of the traffic so that the formation below the pavement can support the weight. The second is to provide a smooth, skid-resistant surface for the traffic.

The strength of a road pavement depends on the strength of the formation – which varies according to the type of soil – and on the type of traffic that will be using it. The formation strength is usually measured by the **Californian Bearing Ratio** (CBR) test. Clays and silts have lower strength values, whereas sand and gravels have higher values.

As a wheel load travels across the pavement it causes a small vertical movement in the pavement and in the formation. Gradually, the cumulative effect of the traffic causes a weakening – known as fatigue – in the pavement and formation, so that cracks, ruts and potholes appear. A road pavement thus has only a limited life.

By far the greatest cause of pavement fatigue is commercial truck traffic with heavy axle loadings of about 8-12 tons. The design of a road pavement is therefore based to a great extent on the number of trucks and their axle loadings expected to use the road over a fixed period or life. This may be anything from five to forty years, after which the pavement will need strengthening or reconstructing.

On minor roads, which are less used by heavy traffic, a crushed stone or gravel-based pavement – a dirt road – will suffice, as long as the surface is regularly inspected and repaired. However, if greater numbers of commercial trucks begin to use the road, routine maintenance becomes expensive. The solution is to lay a bituminous surface dressing which prevents rainwater from seeping into the pavement.

For roads that are designed for heavy and constant use, the pavement construction has to be very strong. There are two main types of structural pavement.

Bituminous pavements
The materials used for making bituminous pavements are crushed stone aggregate and bitumen mixtures. Together they form what is often called asphaltic concrete. Because of a certain plasticity in the material, this form of construction is known as a flexible

Center. An asphalt paver laying a course of a flexible pavement. Notice how the truck is loading the hot asphalt into the paver, which spreads and grades the course as it moves forward. The course is then compacted true to an accurate level by heavy road rollers.

Above. A concrete paving train laying a pavement. Notice how the concrete is being fed sideways to the paver, which, as it moves forward, spreads, compacts and finishes the road surface to an accurate line and level.

pavement.

The subbase provides the working platform on which the upper layers of the pavement are constructed. The top layer – known as the wearing course – is made of a finer material than the base course as it has to withstand traffic wear and tear as well as to provide a smooth, skid-resistant surface.

The aggregate and bitumen are heated and mixed together at an asphalt plant, under carefully-controlled conditions. The asphaltic concrete is then transported to the road site where it is laid by asphalt pavers and compacted by road rollers to the specified line and level.

Concrete pavements

These are made of crushed stone, or of gravel aggregate and Portland cement. Mixed together, they form concrete which is used either unreinforced, or reinforced by a mesh of steel bars. If the steel bars are used, the depth of construction is thinner. This form of construction is known as "rigid."

There are two ways in which a concrete pavement is laid, both are highly mechanized.

Concrete train. Rails on which the train will run are laid alongside both edges of the highway at exactly the same level as the final road surface. As well as carrying the train, the rails also act as temporary **side forms** or molds. The train is fed with concrete, which it spreads, compacts and finishes as it travels slowly along the route. *Slip form paver.* The paver travels on its own tracks over the sub base. The level is controlled by taut wires that are specially erected and fixed alongside the road. Like the train, the paver is fed with concrete, which it spreads, compacts and finishes, but the side forms that retain the concrete are built into (and move with) the paver.

These two construction methods have to be carefully planned and controlled to ensure that the concrete supply can be fed into the train or paver continuously, and that its quality remains the same so that the road surface is uniform.

To allow for shrinkage and thermal movements (expansion and contraction) joints are placed between sections of the concrete. Finally, before the concrete surface has completely set, it is roughened with mechanical steel brushes to give it skid-resistance.

Structures

When a road is built, the obstructions caused both by nature and by man have to be overcome. This is achieved by means of structures such as culverts, bridges, viaducts, tunnels and retaining walls.

The number of structures on a major road can be considerable, particularly when the road is grade-separated. For example, on a 140-mile length of the M1 inter-city motorway in the UK there are some 400 structures. They accounted for just over a quarter of the total cost of the road. In less-developed areas the proportion would not be as high, but in highly built-up urban areas the structures can account for the major proportion of the cost.

Bridges and viaducts
Unlike cuttings and embankments, which blend into their surroundings, bridges and viaducts form a notable architectural feature of any landscape, and each has its own characteristics. This is not only true of the great bridges of the world which span rivers and estuaries. It also applies to many smaller bridges found on modern roads. These smaller bridges are still comparatively large structures, each with its own problems of design and construction.

As many road bridges fulfill a similar function, it is often possible to standardize the form of construction. The detailed differences are the angle at which a bridge or viaduct crosses over the road, and the width, height and gradient of the over-road.

The factors determining the design are the clearance required, the loads that the structure has to carry, and the foundation conditions. Clearance – both in width and height – will depend upon road and rail traffic needs, and river and flood waterways.

The main loads that act on a bridge or viaduct vary according to the type of structure. They include its own weight, traffic loading, wind pressure, earth and ground-water pressure, river-flow effect, and, in certain areas, forces due to earthquakes.

If the ground is strong enough to support the structure at a relatively shallow depth, **spread foundations** are constructed. Where foundations at greater depths are necessary, **piling** may be used to transfer the loads to a stronger soil stratum.

Materials used in the construction vary depending on availability and circumstances: they may be reinforced concrete, prestressed concrete, **structural steel**, or a combination of these materials.

Retaining walls
Retaining walls are mostly used to support

own weight

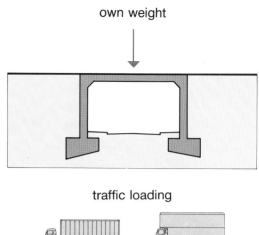

traffic loading

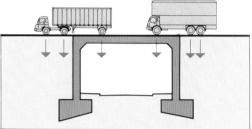

wind pressure

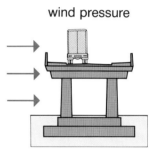

earth and groundwater pressure

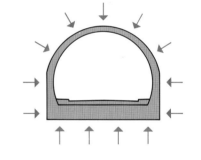

river-flow effect

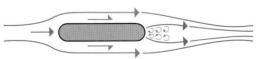

earthquakes

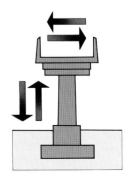

the earth alongside cuttings or in embankments where the area available is not big enough to form a slope – usually because the land was too expensive. Large retaining walls are costly to construct, so when locating the route, the road engineer adjusts the alignment and gradient to reduce their height as much as possible.

Retaining walls are built from many materials including plain and reinforced concrete, natural rock, closely spaced steel or concrete piles or from **reinforced earth**.

Tunnels

Tunnels are very expensive structures. They are generally only built where the depth of the cutting would be excessive or – as in cities and major towns – the land is not available for alternative construction.

There are many types of tunnel but most fall into one of two categories: bored or cut-and-cover. Bored tunnels, used for passing under or through obstacles to the road, often at great depth, are bored out by a tunnelling machine or by blasting and excavation by skilled miners. Cut-and-cover tunnels are only built at shallow depths and constructed by excavating a trench, building the tunnel within it and replacing the ground over it.

Culverts

These carry streams and small watercourses across the road. They vary in size from small pipes of about 3 feet (1 m) in diameter to quite large reinforced concrete or corrugated steel tube structures, rather like small bridges.

Typical bridges carrying existing roads over and under a new major road.

Below. A complicated system of overpasses and underpasses at the intersection of two major expressways (Dallas, Texas).

Signs and Safety

If you have ever lost your way on a small country road because there were no road signs to tell you which way to go, you will know just how important signs and communication systems are. But signs do not just provide directions. They also act as warnings and regulators.

Once that the main civil engineering construction of a new road has been completed, the road has to be made usable for traffic. This entails the installation of road markings, traffic signs, communication systems, safety barriers and lighting – depending upon the type of road it is and its location. At the same time, any necessary landscaping and planting of trees or shrubs can begin, so that in due course the road will blend into its environment.

Traffic signs have three purposes: to regulate, to warn and to inform. They may be markings on the road, traffic signals, roadside signs, or even signs and signals attached to overhead **gantries**.

Regulatory signs are designed to maintain safe standards of driving and to uphold the law. They give notice of any restriction or prohibition on speed, movement and waiting times of

vehicles. For certain roads they also denote the class of vehicles which are allowed to use them.

Warning signs give notice that there are permanent hazards ahead – pedestrian crossings, traffic merging, schools, or temporary hazards such as roadworks or accidents.

Information signs show routes, destinations, facilities and places of interest.

Road markings are used for all three purposes but their main function on the open road is to mark out the driving lanes to ensure that traffic keeps safely in line. Usually, road markings are made of a white reflective thermoplastic material sometimes with reflective road studs to help drivers see them at night and in wet conditions.

Wherever you go in the world, regulatory and warning signs by the side of the road are generally of the same size, shape, color and symbol so that any motorist in a foreign country can understand the regulation or warning.

Information signs, on the other hand, cannot be standardized, but they must be large and clear so that a driver can read them at a distance. As signs must not be too large, the information has to be limited to important destinations.

It can be quite difficult to find the right site for information signs. On large highways with several lanes, a sign at the side of the road may not be visible from the center lanes, so such signs are mounted on gantries above the road.

At night, traffic signs are lit by reflectors or lights. Lights are especially needed over signs when the surrounding area is illuminated: for instance, street lighting in towns that would throw shadows across unlit signs making them impossible to read.

Sometimes temporary traffic signs or warnings are needed – temporary lane controls, speed restrictions, or diversions. On modern roads carrying heavy traffic, variable warning signs have been introduced in the form of a dot-matrix display, controlled by a microprocessor operated from a computerized control center.

On major roads, or in remote areas where there is a great distance between interchanges, a communication system for reporting breakdowns or accidents has to be provided. This is usually a telephone system with call boxes at about one mile intervals along the route. Refreshment and service facilities are also needed at regular intervals, some 12-50 miles along the road, depending on the volume of traffic.

Where roads carry a great deal of traffic, and in urban areas, lighting has to be installed for safety reasons. Concrete or steel safety barriers are often needed on divided highways to prevent traffic from crossing onto an opposite lane and hitting oncoming traffic. Similar types of barriers are erected to provide protection from hazards such as bridge piers and sign gantries. Parapets or safety fences are provided at the sides of roads across bridges, viaducts or high embankments.

Opposite. Illuminated direction sign mounted on an overhead gantry above a busy highway.

Right. An unusual warning sign – for Australia only! (Nullarbor Plain, Western Australia).

Below. Safety fence installed to contain vehicles on an embankment and at a sharp curve in the road. The photograph shows a truck-mounted auger used for boring the holes for the safety fence posts (Wyoming).

Road Management and Maintenance

Once construction has been completed and the road has been opened to traffic, it cannot be left to look after itself. It has to be checked at regular intervals for wear and tear from traffic and weather, and for damage caused by accidents and by severe weather, such as storms. When necessary, repairs must be carried out as quickly as possible to ensure that the road is safe for traffic.

The responsibility lies with a road management organization, which operates a planned maintenance system. The system defines the standards to which the various parts of the road should be maintained, and specifies when regular inspections should take place. Usually the organization responsible is a central or local government road authority but for toll road systems a special authority is normally set up. The authority will be responsible for the inspection, design, programming and supervision of maintenance work, which is carried out either by the authority's work force or by contractors.

There are two kinds of road maintenance, both of which are concerned with keeping the road in a good condition for the safe and economical passage of traffic.

Routine maintenance

The most immediate problems are dealt with regularly. The road has to be kept clean, free of litter and debris from vehicles, and from dirt and mud carried on to it from nearby building sites or land. Other routine activities are clearing the road drainage gullies and channels, and repairing damage caused by traffic accidents or storms to the road pavement, signs, lighting, barrier rails, bridge parapets, noise barriers and fencing.

Repairs to local defects in the road pavement – such as potholes – are carried out. Curbs, embankments, cutting slopes and landscaped areas are mown and maintained. When conditions are icy the road is salted or gritted, snow is cleared and, in desert regions, drifting sand is swept from the road.

Occasional emergency works caused by, say, ground collapse, flooding or a road accident, are also dealt with by routine maintenance.

Capital maintenance

Longer-term requirements involve reports and inspections of the road elements – the pavement, structures, earthworks, drainage – at regular intervals to monitor its condition. A forecast can then be made of when and where a program of repairs or reconstruction will be needed.

For example, by inspecting and testing the road pavement and by taking into account the records of the traffic that it has carried, a forecast can be made of when it will need to be strengthened. If heavy traffic uses the road constantly, pavement strengthening or reconstruction has to be carefully planned. Traffic diversions and signs must be set up, temporary safety measures installed, and a program of works drawn up to avoid serious traffic delays.

Without maintenance a road can very quickly become "unmade"!

Heavy traffic such as this creates great problems in carrying out maintenance work (Harbor Freeway, Los Angeles).

Winter maintenance; keeping the road clear of snow is a major requirement in colder countries.

Repairing temperature-induced cracking. This may be caused by extremes of heat and cold (Wyoming, US).

The photograph shows the operation of traffic control on a busy highway (45,000 vehicles per day). In this case it is to provide working space for reconstruction of the drainage. (M18 Motorway, UK).

Facts and Figures

The mileage of public authority controlled roads throughout the world as recorded by the International Road Federation in Geneva, is just over 12,000,000 miles. However, these records do not include roads in every country, in particular roads in China and the USSR, so the total world mileage of roads is probably as much as 15,000,000 miles, the equivalent of a road circling the Earth over 600 times.

The recorded mileage can be broken down into the number of road miles for each continent.

	Miles
North America	4,050,000
Europe	2,680,000
Asia and the Middle East	2,295,000
Latin America	1,661,000
Africa	808,000
Australasia	590,000

Examined in even greater detail – country by country – the recorded road mileage gives a clear picture of the relationship of roads to local population, settlement patterns, development and geography.

In a relatively small country like the UK with a proportionally large urban population, the density of road usage is high. On the other hand, in a big country like the US, the long stretches of road in comparatively under-populated areas such as the Midwest, result in much lower average road usage per mile.

	LAND AREA '000 sq. miles	POPULATION '000,000 (approx.)
UNITED STATES	3615	244
CANADA	3561	27
BRAZIL	3285	141
FRANCE	213	56
WEST GERMANY	96	61
UNITED KINGDOM	89	57
ITALY	116	57
ZAMBIA	290	7
SAUDI ARABIA	870	14
THAILAND	198	54
JAPAN	146	122
AUSTRALIA	2966	16

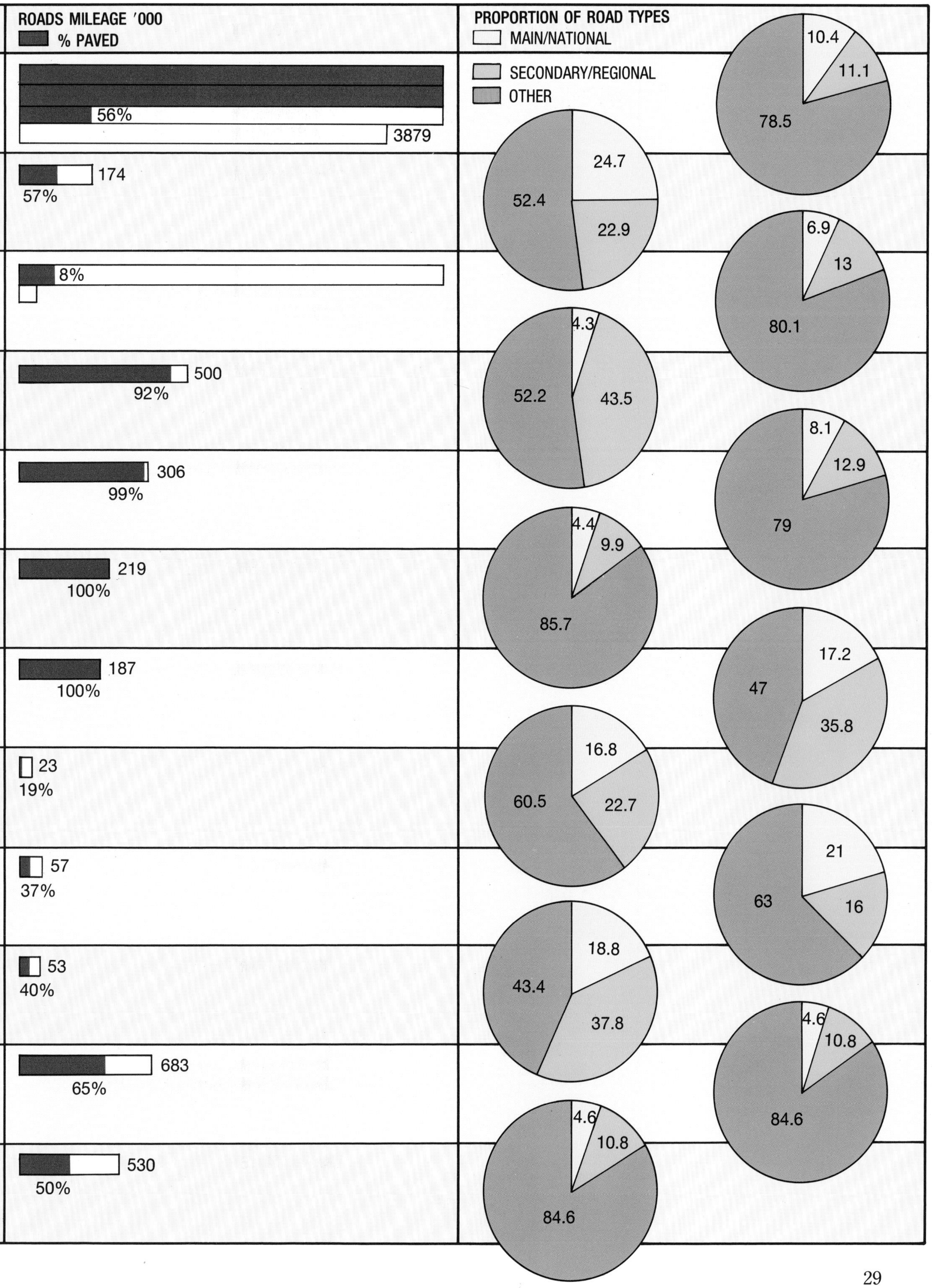
ROADS MILEAGE '000
% PAVED
56%
3879
174
57%
8%
500
92%
306
99%
219
100%
187
100%
23
19%
57
37%
53
40%
683
65%
530
50%
PROPORTION OF ROAD TYPES
MAIN/NATIONAL
SECONDARY/REGIONAL
OTHER
10.4
11.1
78.5
24.7
22.9
52.4
6.9
13
80.1
4.3
43.5
52.2
8.1
12.9
79
4.4
9.9
85.7
17.2
35.8
47
16.8
22.7
60.5
21
16
63
18.8
37.8
43.4
4.6
10.8
84.6
4.6
10.8
84.6

Earthmoving Equipment

The **bulldozer** shown is equipped with a large blade for spreading and leveling earthworks. At the rear is a ripper for breaking up soft rock formations. This machine weighs about 50 tons. Bulldozers are often used to assist other machines, such as the scraper shown below.

The pneumatic tired **scraper** shown is mainly used for excavating, transporting and spreading earthworks material to form cuttings and embankments. It can carry 34 tons and normally operates over distances of around a quarter of a mile.

The tracked **excavator** illustrated is equipped with a 100 cubic foot bucket and is capable of digging to a depth of 26 feet (8 meters). This type of machine is used for deep trenching, general excavation and loading material into trucks for transportation.

The articulated **dump truck** shown carries a maximum load of 22.5 tons. This type of vehicle is used to move excavated earthworks along often considerable lengths of a road construction site. Larger dump trucks commonly used on roadworks can move loads of about 75 tons at a time.

30

Glossary

Aggregates Crushed rock, gravel and sand used in concretes and asphalts.

Alignment Geometrical positioning – horizontal and vertical – of a line, usually the center line, along a road to provide curvatures and gradients.

Asphalt A mixture of bituminous material and aggregates used in road pavement construction.

Bedrock Hard rock lying under weaker surface soils.

Bitumen A viscous or solid mixture of hydrocarbons that occurs naturally, or is obtained by distillation of petroleum. It is used as a binder in the surfacing of road pavements.

Californian Bearing Ratio (CBR) A test for assessing the strength of soils by comparing their behavior with that of a standard material.

Channel System A system of drainage using open channels.

Concrete A mixture of Portland cement and aggregates that hardens as it sets. It has considerable strength in compression but little in tension. To give it tensile strength it is reinforced with steel rods (reinforced concrete) or put into compression by high-tensile steel wires (prestressed concrete).

Cutting An excavation for a road below ground level.

Design Speed The nominal speed of traffic on a road, which is used to determine the geometrical alignment standards for curvature, gradients, etc.

Digital Ground Model (DGM) A mathematical model of the ground surface and its features.

Earthworks The excavation of cuttings and the haul, placing and compaction of the excavated fill in embankments; or the disposal of it elsewhere.

EDM System Electromagnetic instruments using infra red or microwave rays for rapid and accurate measurement of distances.

Embankment A bank of soil or rock built up above ground level to carry a road.

Fill Soil or rock excavated in cuttings, or obtained elsewhere.

Flexible Pavement *See* Road Pavement.

Formation The top surface of finished earthworks that has been prepared to receive the pavement construction.

Gantry A light bridge of steel or concrete suspended over a road to support road signs and signals.

Geometric Computation The calculation of the precise position of points along the alignment of a road.

Geometrical Alignment *See* Alignment.

Geotechnical Relating to the study of soil and rocks for engineering purposes.

Gradient The upward or downward slope of a road as it rises and falls.

Ground Form The shape of the ground surface, from which geological assessment can ascertain whether landslides and similar movements may occur.

Hydraulic Pressure Loadings The loads imposed on structures by water in the surrounding soil.

Infrared Light An electromagnetic radiation that has a wave-length longer than that of visible light but shorter than that of radio waves.

Lacustrine Soils deposited under lakes.

Microwaves Electromagnetic radiation of wavelengths between 0.001 and 0.3 meters.

Pavement *See* Road Pavement.

Piling Concrete, steel or timber columns driven through weak ground to provide a foundation on stronger ground at a depth to which it would not be economical to excavate. (*See* Spread footings.)

Pipe Surface and subsoil water is conveyed by pipes or open channels to suitable outlets.

Proctor Test A test carried out in a laboratory to measure the density of a compacted soil sample.

Reinforced Earth A method of strengthening fill material by embedding in it tensile reinforcing elements (e.g. metal or plastic strips) attached to a permanent facing to form a vertical wall.

Retaining Wall A wall constructed to support earth or other solid material.

Right-of-way The strip of land on which a road is built.

Ripper A tractor with a rear downward-pointing, steel toothed attachment.

Road Pavement The whole road construction, from the surface down to the formation. Concrete pavements are referred to as "rigid" pavements. Asphalt pavements are referred to as "flexible" pavements.

Scraper A large, box-shaped bucket excavator on heavy, tired wheels, towed by a tractor. When the bucket's blade is lowered, its movement over the ground scrapes the soil into the bucket.

Settlement The downward movement of soil due to compression caused by applied loading or in an embankment by its own weight.

Side Forms Edges supporting a concrete pavement during construction.

Sight Line The distance, without fixed obstacles, which a driver can see ahead. It must be sufficient to allow time for the driver to take appropriate action.

Spread Foundation A foundation – square, rectangular, circular – large enough to spread the load of the structure which it is supporting.

Stereoscopic Plotter A plotting instrument that enables stereoscopic pairs of photographs to be viewed, so that maps and plans can be prepared from them.

Stopping distance The distance a vehicle travels from braking to stopping.

Structural Steel Rolled steel beams and columns or fabricated steel sections, joined together by bolting, welding or riveting.

Surveyor's Level An instrument with a telescope and bubble level which enables level sights to be taken over considerable distances. It is used for measuring differences in height from point to point.

Theodolite Sometimes called a 'transit', this is a surveying instrument for measuring horizontal and vertical angles.

Topography The detailed description of the surface features of an area.

Trigonometrical Station A survey station (or point on the earth's surface) whose position has been accurately determined.

Viaduct A road bridge spanning a stretch of countryside where an embankment would be uneconomical.

Walkover Survey A preliminary survey conducted on foot to determine the extent of detail which will be required in the main survey.

Index

Acknowledgments

Threshold Books and the publishers gratefully acknowledge the
help given in the production of this book by Laurie Hopkins of
Sir Owen Williams and Partners. We would also like to thank
Stephen Everton of R.M. Douglas Construction Ltd and
Christopher Unwin of John Laing plc.

Illustration credits
Photographs: Asset International Ltd 19 (right); Philip Cornwell
8; R.M. Douglas Construction Limited Front cover, 20, 30 (top
and centre); Fugro McLelland Limited 14 (bottom); Sir Alexander
Gibb & Partners 3 (top), 19 (left); John Downman/Hutchinson
Library 3 (top), 25 (top); Paul van Riel/Robert Harding Picture
Library 26; John Laing plc 13, 21, 30 (bottom); Department of
Main Roads NSW, Australia 17; Nihon Doro Kodan 5 (bottom);
Crown copyright reserved, reproduced by kind permission of
Ordnance Survey 9, 10, 11, 12; copyright Shuel-Sha Publishing
House 5 (top); F.H.C. Birch 27 (top) G.R. Richardson/Spectrum
Colour Library 24; State Department of Highways, Austin, Texas
23 (bottom); Sir Owen Williams & Partners 14 (top), 23 (top and
centre), 27 (bottom); US Department of Transportation 4
(bottom); Wyoming State Highways Department 25 (bottom), 27
(centre); K. Benser/ZEFA Picture Library 4.

Diagrams and drawings: John Hutchinson 2, 4 (bottom), 6, 7, 12
(bottom), 15, 16, 17, 18, 22; Eddie Poulton 4 (top), 20, 28, 29.

Picture research: Celia Dearing.

Facts On File, Inc.
460 Park Avenue South
New York NY 10016
USA

Library of Congress Cataloging-in-Publication Data

Williams, Owen, 1916–
    How roads are made/text, Owen Williams; design, Eddie Poulton.
    32 p. 30 × 21 cm. (How it is made).
    Includes index.
    Summary: Provides a detailed description of all stages of road making
and considers the important element of traffic.
    ISBN 0-8160-2041-8.
    1. Roads—Design and construction—Juvenile literature.
[1. Roads—Design and construction.] I. Poulton, Eddie.
II. Title. III. Series.
TE149.W55   1989
625.7—dc20   89-31330 CIP   AC

Facts On File books are available at special discounts when purchased
in bulk quantities for businesses, associations, institutions or sales
promotion. Please contact the Special Sales Department of our New York
office at 212/683-2244 (dial 800/322-8755 except in NY, AK or HI).

General Editor: Barbara Cooper.
Design by Eddie Poulton.
Composition by Rapid Communications Ltd, London, England.
Printed in England by Maclehose & Partners, Portsmouth.

10 9 8 7 6 5 4 3 2 1